Sanctuary for Sensitivity

Transforming Sensitivity To Strength

By Shenita Sanders

Copyright © 2024

All rights reserved. No part of this book may be reproduced or transmitted without express permission in writing from the author.

The information contained in this book is for general information purposes only and should not be considered a substitute for the advice of a mental health professional.

To be a sensitive person is to carry the weight of the world in your heart while illuminating it with the light of your soul. It is to feel deeply, love fiercely, and navigate life with an extraordinary capacity for empathy and compassion.

Introduction

"I was cast aside, dismissed, and told my sensitive feelings were too much to handle. That rejection led me to find love within myself and become my own heroine." Shenita Sanders

Welcome to your sanctuary. In the sanctuary, you will enjoy a tranquil, safe haven to just be. A sacred space to feel accepted and supported unconditionally. This is your 30-day journey toward a more empowering and vibrant way of being. This guided journal is specially crafted for individuals who desire to successfully navigate profound feelings of sensitivity and empathy with strength and vigor. During your time in the Sanctuary for Sensitivity, you will embark on a healing journey of self-awareness and deep connection. You will see yourself through the eyes of love and compassion and finally come to understand that your feelings are not a curse but instead an abundant source of creative power.

Imagine being a powerful wi-fi signal. Your strong signal is fast, supports any device, and is excellent at receiving or downloading large data packets. Most importantly, your signal is incredibly reliable. Your wi-fi service has an excellent reputation for always succeeding in the toughest spots. Zero dropped connections. Your wi-fi signal always runs at full strength.

Now like everything else, you notice you're running slower than normal. You're not processing commands as quickly. This happens more frequently, and reboots are not helping you to bounce back as quickly as before. Let's do some troubleshooting to restore your signal back to running at full speed.

While taking a closer look, you notice your signal is being blocked by too many walls and you're too far from any window. You also realize that the signals of other wi-fi devices are interfering with your ability to function properly. You simply are working harder than necessary and the much needed adjustments are welcomed.

Your solution is simple, it involves getting away from unnecessary walls, getting as close to windows as possible, and significantly reducing outside interference of other wi-fi devices. Perfect. Now, you are back operating at full strength. You have a better understanding of how strong you are and what you need to operate under ideal conditions. You're motivated to do what works best to keep yourself running at optimum speeds.

As sensitive beings, we are a fine-tuned signal. We were born with the gift of empathy and a special ability to deeply connect to the feelings of others. We carry an invisible signal that attracts others and allows them to feel at ease with us. Encouraging words help us to feel invincible, conversely, harsh words directed at us can feel like a knife in the heart. There are times when it's hard to disconnect from people and their struggles. We are incredibly perceptive, quickly processing information that most people miss, but that causes us to overanalyze things at times. We get lost in our feelings and often assume burdens that are not ours to carry.

When we walk into a room, we physically absorb all its energy. Big crowds and noises send us running for dear life in the other direction. It's sensory overload. Everything feels so heightened and chaotic. We try to explain it to others, but not many people understand the crushing anxiety we feel on the inside. We desperately long for empathy from others, but instead, often experience rejection. The inevitable judgement of being broken, too dramatic, or weird. Our sensitivity can make us feel alone and isolated. It feels exhausting being dismissed and told to toughen up or grow up. Our sensitive nature requires a lot of mental and emotional energy to do the simple things that most people take for granted. We spend a lot of energy searching for more peace and desperately wanting to be understood.

During your time in the sanctuary, you'll discover daily grounding and soul-searching exercises that will start to increase your emotional strength. Inside you will find a quote of the day, reflection prompt, daily intentions and action suggestions, a gratitude tip, and two process days. I have also included extra pages for note-taking in the back.

My intention for this guided journal is to help you delve deeply into your emotional landscape and uncover your hidden strength buried within your sensitive nature.

With a loving and compassionate approach, you'll become more in-tune with your emotions and learn how to successfully navigate the world with greater confidence and ease. At the end of your sacred journey, my prayer is that you will transform into a more dynamic version of yourself and take ownership of a superpower that is often misunderstood by others. Your sensitivity is not a weakness; it's a form of strength that when harnessed, can make you a more compassionate, intuitive, and resilient being. Your time in the Sanctuary for Sensitivity will teach you how to take your superhuman abilities and have them work for you and not against you. To have safe and respectful relationships with others. More importantly, you will grow to have a safe and respectful relationship with yourself. You will learn how to tap into the wise and infinite power of your inner guidance and become to yourself how you desire to relate to others.

I encourage you to always see yourself through the eyes of love and compassion. Open yourself to any insights that your inner guidance shares along your sacred journey. Allow yourself to listen without judgement and follow through accordingly with love.

My desire for you is to embrace and find joy in your sensitive nature, to master your emotions, and ultimately learn how to show up unapologetically in relationships. It took a lot of practice for me to discover that getting good rest (not just sleep), spending quiet time in nature, having healthier boundaries, and sound therapy are the best tools in my emotional wellness routine. I had to learn how to make myself a priority without guilt. That first came with having many honest conversations with myself. I learned how to take accountability and responsibility for my sensitivity. I began listening without judgment and acknowledging any needs that presented themselves. As my brother Mario taught me many years ago, "You can't heal until you get real." His wise words put me on my path to healing, and now I enjoy a loving and affirming relationship with myself.

Following the format of my previous guided journal, Navigating Boundaries, there is no wrong way to complete your journey. You are encouraged to create a special sanctuary. A sacred space where you feel enticed to visit without interruption during your daily practice. A place where you show up each day with the joyful anticipation of discovering new ways to better appreciate yourself. Allowing gratitude to encourage you and become your fuel for future success.

I'm proud of you for taking this courageous step. Together, let's embark on your epic journey. May inspiration, comfort, and encouragement be your constant companions. Here's to embracing your sacred sensitivity, celebrating your empathy, and discovering the resilient and powerful soul within you.

Welcome to your sacred journey.

Welcome to living life with greater confidence and ease my beautiful sensitive friend.

Acknowledgements

To my dearest Margie. Thank you for being my light and encouraging me. Your love allows me to blossom in beautiful and vibrant ways. I never knew abundance until you came into my life. I am forever grateful that you are my best friend and love me to life. MORE!

Date: _____

My intention(s) for starting this journey is…

_____
_____
_____
_____
_____
_____
_____
_____
_____
_____
_____
_____
_____
_____
_____
_____
_____
_____
_____
_____
_____

Week 1: Understanding Your Sensitivity

Whether you are highly responsive to social or environmental stimuli or highly intuitive and absorb all the energy in a room, the overwhelming feeling you experience is the bridge that connects empaths and highly sensitive people.

This week, you will unlock the door to a deeper self-awareness and acceptance. Sensitivity is often seen as a liability, but it is, in fact, a profound strength- a unique lens through which to see, experience, and interpret the world. Embracing your sensitivity will allow you to harness the depth of your experiences and use them to safely navigate life with purpose and strength.

Your sacred journey is not about seeing yourself as broken or weak but rather about cultivating more appreciation and respect for your beautiful, sensitive heart.

You got this!

Day 1   Date: _____

Understanding Your Sensitivity

"We are a package deal. Our trait of sensitivity means we will also be cautious, inward, needing extra time alone. Because people without the trait (the majority) do not understand that, they see us as timid, shy, weak, or that greatest sin of all, unsociable. Fearing these labels, we try to be like others. But that leads to our becoming overaroused and distressed. Then that gets us labeled neurotic or crazy, first by others and then by ourselves." Elaine Aron, PhD

Reflection Prompt:

Describe a time when you felt overwhelmed by your surroundings. What were the circumstances, and how did you handle it?

Daily Intentions and Actions:
- Intention: Set an intention to be kind to yourself today.
- Action: Plan a 10-minute walk in a quiet setting.

Gratitude Tip: Write down 3 things you are grateful for.

Day 1   Date: _____

Day 2   Date: _____

Embrace Your Gifts

"One of my favorite aspects of high sensitivity is finding wonder in the smallest things." Cati Vanden Breul

Reflection Prompt:

List several ways your sensitivity has given you an advantage in your relationships.

Daily Intentions and Actions:
- Intention: See your sensitivity as a strength.
- Action: Write a thank you note to yourself for the ways your sensitive nature brings you joy.

Gratitude Tip: Express gratitude for sensitivity and how it enhances your life .

Day 2

Date: _____

Day 3   Date: _____

Identifying Triggers

"Highly sensitive people learned early in life to try to control the external world as a way to attempt to manage their inner one." Sheryl Paul

Reflection Prompt:

Reflect on your daily routine and identify times when you experience feelings of stress or overwhelm.

Daily Intentions and Actions:
- Intention: Compassionately observe your interactions and reactions with others.
- Action: Start a trigger diary and provide appropriate details.

Gratitude Tip: Express gratitude for the gift of self-awareness and how you will use it on your journey.

Day 3

Date: _____

Day 4   Date: _____

Self-Care Strategies

"Sensitive people like a slower pace of life. We like pondering all our options before making a decision and regularly reflecting on our experiences. We hate busy schedules and rushing from one event to the next."
Jenn Granneman

Reflection Prompt:

What self-care practices help you to feel grounded and calm?

Daily Intentions and Actions:
- Intention: Set an intention to prioritize your emotional wellbeing.
- Action: Design a meaningful self-care routine that honors your sensitivity journey.

Gratitude Tip: Be mindful of the small moments of peace during your day and be thankful.

Day 4

Date: _____

Day 5

Date: _____

Boundaries

"Meaningful boundaries are my soul's way of saying, "I am worth protecting." I know I'm extraordinary, and so is my sensitivity and the light it brings to the world." Shenita Sanders

Reflection Prompt:

Think of a time when you successfully set a boundary. How did it impact your emotional wellbeing?

Daily Intentions and Actions:
- Intention: Set an intention to honor your boundaries.
- Action: Take an honest inventory of your boundaries. Make any necessary adjustments that will cultivate a deeper level of self-respect.

Gratitude Tip: Give thanks for boundaries and how they have improved the way you relate to yourself and others.

Day 5

Date: _____

Day 6

Date: _____

Energy Management

"They hear nearly every sound, notice every movement, and process the expression on every person's face. And that means that simply walking through a public space can be an assault on their senses." Andre Sólo (discussing hsp's)

Reflection Prompt:

What situations drain your energy levels the most? How do you recharge your emotional battery?

Daily Intentions and Actions:
- Intention: Set an intention to closely monitor your energy levels.
- Action: Get creative with fun ways to recharge your energy.

Gratitude Tip: Honor one activity that faithfully recharges your energy.

Day 6

Date: _____

Day 7

Date: _____

Mindful Reflection

"The journey of a thousand miles begins with one step." Lao Tzu

Reflection Prompt:

Reflect on what you have learned this week. What insight has been the most beneficial?

Daily Intentions and Actions:
- Intention: Take time to acknowledge your progress.
- Action: Write a journal entry of what worked well for you this week and what support you need to continue your positive momentum.

Gratitude Tip: Express gratitude for who you are now and the empowered, sensitive being you are becoming.

Day 7

Date: _____

Week 2:

Emotional Mastery

Welcome back dear friend. I'm so proud of you for getting through your first week and showing up to learn more. By learning to navigate your emotions skillfully, you gain the ability to remain grounded and centered amidst the ebbs and flows of life.

This week, we will focus on emotional mastery. Understanding your sensitive nature and mastering your emotions empowers you to maneuver various situations with clarity and ease rather than being swept away by intense emotions. It helps you establish healthier boundaries, manage stress, and make thoughtful decisions, all essential for maintaining your well-being. Ultimately, emotional mastery allows you to connect more deeply with yourself, foster satisfying relationships, and live a more balanced and fulfilling life.

Day 8   Date: _____

Emotional Awareness

"Everything I experience hits me deep, raw, and intense. As an empath, I feel the energy of myself and others. As I age, this ability only grows deeper and stranger."
Sylvester McNutt III

Reflection Prompt:

Describe your current emotional state. What emotions are most prominent? How do they impact your behavior?

Daily Intentions and Actions:
- Intention: Take time to observe your emotions.
- Action: Enjoy a 5-minute mindfulness meditation. Become aware of any changes in your emotional state.

Gratitude Tip: Be thankful for the emotions that support you.

Day 8

Date: _____

Day 9

Date: _____

Emotional Regulation

"Emotions are not problems to be solved. They are signals to be interpreted." Vironika Tugaleva

Reflection Prompt:

What are your strategies for managing difficult emotions? Are they effective? What adjustments do you need to make?

Daily Intentions and Actions:
- Intention: Become aware of your emotions and enlist the appropriate level of support.
- Action: Try something new, like sound therapy, and reflect on its effectiveness.

Gratitude Tip: Appreciate a moment when you successfully managed your emotions.

Day 9

Date: _____

Day 10

Date: _____

Understanding Empathy

"The real warriors in this world are the ones that see the details of another's soul." Shannon L. Alder

Reflection Prompt:

How does empathy show up in your interactions with others? How does empathy show up for your needs?

Daily Intentions and Actions:

- Intention: Consciously practice empathy for yourself.
- Action: Recall a meaningful experience when you experienced empathy from others.

Gratitude Tip: Express gratitude for the gift of understanding others and feeling understood.

Day 10

Date: _____

Day 11

Date: _____

Handling Emotional Overload

"My message for everyone is the same: that if we can learn to identify, express, and harness our feelings, even the most challenging ones, we can use those emotions to help us create positive, satisfying lives." Marc Brackett

Reflection Prompt:

Are you effective in recognizing your emotional overload? What patterns or triggers do you notice?

Daily Intentions and Actions:

- Intention: Be mindful of your body's signals of overload.
- Action: Create a list of triggers and compassionate strategies to manage your emotions.

Gratitude Tip: Appreciate your ability to recognize and protect yourself from emotional overload.

Day 11

Date: _____

Day 12

Date: _____

Emotional Boundaries

"When you notice someone does something toxic the first time, don't wait for the second time before you address it or cut them off. Many survivors are used to the "wait and see" tactic which only leaves them vulnerable to a second attack. As your boundaries get stronger, the wait time gets shorter. You never have to justify your intuition." Shahida Arabi

Reflection Prompt:

How does other people's negative emotions impact you? How do you handle it?

Daily Intentions and Actions:

- Intention: Be assertive and protect your emotional space.
- Action: Practice setting emotional boundaries and notice your thoughts, feelings, and outcomes.

Gratitude Tip: Express gratitude for your growing emotional strength.

Day 12   Date: _____

Day 13

Date: _____

Cultivating Joy

"Joy is not in things. It's in us."
Richard Wagner

Reflection Prompt:

What activities, people, or moments bring joy to your life? What tools or support do you need to make cultivating joy a daily practice?

Daily Intentions and Actions:

- Intention: Set an intention to create joyful moments.
- Action: Create a meaningful plan to incorporate more joy into your daily routine.

Gratitude Tip: Express gratitude for the joy that shows up in your life.

Day 13   Date: _____

Day 14

Date: _____

Mindful Reflection

"Reflection is the lamp of the heart. If it departs, the heart will have no light."   Imam Al-Haddad

Reflection Prompt:

What new emotional insights have you gained this week? How have they helped you to understand yourself better?

Daily Intentions and Actions:

- Intention: Set an intention to honor your emotional journey.
- Action: Summarize your emotional journey and set supportive goals for next week.

Gratitude Tip: Express gratitude for your time in the sanctuary and the emotional growth you are experiencing.

Day 14

Date: _____

Day 15

Date: _____

Process Day

"As important as it is to have a plan for doing work, it is perhaps more important to have a plan for rest, relaxation, self-care, and sleep." Akiroq Brost

Today is a good opportunity to practice the art of rest. You have worked so diligently on developing your strength muscles and have earned a reward. Celebrate this beautiful milestone by doing something special for yourself or nothing at all. You are empowered to honor yourself in whatever way you choose.

At the end of the day, recall any thoughts, feelings, or insights that come up. Examine how they are important to your journey and continue to encourage yourself for continued progress.

Day 15

Date: _____

Week 3: Thriving In Relationships

Welcome to week 3. I hope you enjoyed your day of rest. You're halfway through your sacred sensitivity to strength journey. It's exciting to know that you remain committed to your personal growth and empowerment. Kudos to you!

This week, we will focus on thriving in relationships. You have done a wonderful job of understanding your sensitivity and mastering your emotions. This week is your opportunity to put all your beautiful work to practice. You will gain valuable insights into what support you'll need to protect your peace and enjoy mutually respectful relationships.

Continue to see yourself through the eyes of love and compassion. Your time in the sanctuary is healing and helps you to grow stronger each day. Allow yourself to push past any resistance and know beyond any doubt that you are a powerful and resilient being.

Day 16   Date: _____

Understanding Your Relationship Patterns

"We don't meet people by accident. They are meant to cross our paths for a reason."   Unknown

Reflection Prompt:

Reflect on patterns you notice in your relationships. What insights have you gained? How have they helped you to understand yourself better?

Daily Intentions and Actions:

- Intention: Set an intention to honor the ways you show up in relationships.
- Action: Create fun ways you can better support yourself.

Gratitude Tip: Express gratitude for who you are and the person you are becoming.

Day 16

Date: _____

Day 17   Date: _____

Communication Skills

"But in every circumstance, they (hsp's) communicate eloquently and prodigiously through body language. They constantly send out signals that they are overwhelmed or uncomfortable in your presence or by a particular environment.
Nathan Falde

Reflection Prompt:

How do you use your words or body to communicate your feelings or needs with others? Is it effective? Why or why not?

Daily Intentions and Actions:

- Intention: Notice how you use your body to communicate.
- Action: Practice assertive communication with words.

Gratitude Tip: Express gratitude for moments when you successfully communicated your feelings.

Day 17

Date: _____

Day 18

Date: _____

Navigating Conflict

"No matter who it is or how comfortable you are with someone, when anyone yells at you or talks down to you, you immediately erupt in tears." Lauren Jarvis-Gibson

Reflection Prompt:

How do you handle conflict? Is your approach effective? What skills would you need to learn or improve?

Daily Intentions and Actions:

- Intention: Practice grounding techniques daily for self-care.
- Action: List grounding techniques that can help you better navigate conflicts.

Gratitude Tip: Express gratitude for times of successful conflict resolution and the growth you expereienced.

Day 18

Date: _____

Day 19   Date: _____

Building Supportive Networks

"Surround yourself with only people who are going to lift you higher." Oprah Winfrey

Reflection Prompt:

Who are the people in your life who understand and support you consistently? What characteristics do you look for in a safe, supportive relationship?

Daily Intentions and Actions:

- Intention: Set an intention to nurture your support system.
- Action: Reach out to a supportive person and let them know the value they add to your life.

Gratitude Tip: Express gratitude for each supportive person in your life and how they uniquely contribute to your emotional well-being.

Day 19

Date: _____

Day 20

Date: _____

Self-Compassion in Relationships

"Compassion isn't some kind of self-improvement project or ideal that we're trying to live up to. Having compassion starts and ends with having compassion for all those unwanted parts of ourselves, all those imperfections that we don't even want to look at."
Pema Chodon

Reflection Prompt:

Reflect on ways you are compassionate towards yourself. Do you practice self-compassion consistently? Why or Why not?

Daily Intentions and Actions:

- Intentions: Practice compassionate language when talking about yourself.
- Action: Create fun ways to practice self-compassion daily.

Gratitude Tip: Express gratitude for ways you currently show kindness to yourself.

Day 20

Date: _____

Day 21

Date: _____

Enhancing Intimacy

"Intimacy is about truth. When you realize you can tell someone your truth, when you can show yourself to them, when you stand in front of them and their response is 'you're safe with me', that's intimacy. Taylor Jenkins Reid

Reflection Prompt:

What does intimacy mean to you? How do you create intimacy within yourself and your relationships?

Daily Intentions and Actions:

- Intentions: Create meaningful ways to make deep connections with others.
- Action: Engage in a meaningful conversation with a close friend or partner.

Gratitude Tip: Express gratitude for moments of deep connection in your relationships.

Day 21

Date: _____

Day 22

Date: _____

Mindful Reflection

"We do not learn from experience. We learn from reflecting on experience." John Dewey

Reflection Prompt:

What have you learned about yourself and your relationships this week? How does your sensitivity impact your relationships? What adjustments are you willing to make?

Daily Intentions and Actions:

- Intentions: Set an intention to honor your growth during your journey.
- Action: Practice assertive communication with safe and supportive people.

Gratitude Tip: Express gratitude for the relationships that acknowledge and honor your sensitivity.

Day 22

Date: _____

Week 4: Empowerment and Growth

Can you believe we are in the home stretch of your journey? I hope you are enjoying every minute of your time in the sanctuary. You are an exceptional being, and I am so proud of you for getting this far.

This week, we will focus on two key themes: empowerment and growth. Empowerment allows you to take charge of your life and make choices that reflect your true self. Growth, on the other hand, is about learning from your experiences and becoming a better version of yourself. Together, these themes will offer you a more meaningful way to appreciate your sensitivities.

Now, let's turn our attention to wrapping up this journey with strength and intention. Completing your sacred sensitivity to strength journey is not just about reaching the finish line. It's about integrating what you have learned and applying it to your life moving forward. You've taken significant steps, and it's crucial to recognize them as part of your overall growth. Take a moment to acknowledge and appreciate yourself.

Day 23

Date: _____

Personal Power

"You have power over your mind- not outside events. Realize this, and you will find strength." Marcus Aurelius

Reflection Prompt:

Describe a time when your sensitivities allowed you to feel powerful. Discover any insights that can help you move forward during challenging moments.

Daily Intentions and Actions:

- Intentions: Set an intention to approach your day from a place of power.
- Action: Identify activities that make you feel powerful.

Gratitude Tip: Be thankful for moments when you felt powerful.

Day 23

Date: _____

Day 24

Date: _____

Self-Expression

"To be yourself in a world that is constantly trying to make you something else is the greatest accomplishment." Ralph Waldo Emerson

Reflection Prompt:

How do you express your true self in your daily life? What are some creative ways you can share more of yourself and form deeper connections with safe people?

Daily Intentions and Actions:

- Intentions: Set an intention to communicate your authentic self.
- Action: Create fun moments that represent your authentic self.

Gratitude Tip: Express gratitude for the ability to express your authentic self.

Day 24

Date: _____

Day 25

Date: _____

Overcoming Fear

"When you come out of a storm you won't be the same person that walked in. That's what the storm is all about." — Haruki Murakami

Reflection Prompt:

How does fear hold you back? What support do you need to overcome your fears?

Daily Intentions and Actions:

- Intentions: Set an intention to face a fear.
- Action: Create a list of tips or tools to help you overcome fear.

Gratitude Tip: Express gratitude for the ways you demonstrate courage.

Day 25

Date: _____

Day 26

Date: _____

Vision for the Future

"Your vision will become clear only when you can look into your own heart. Who looks outside, dreams; who looks inside, awakes." Carl Jung

Reflection Prompt:

What is your vision for a strong, vibrant, and empowered life?

Daily Intentions and Actions:

- Intentions: Set an intention to imagine, create, and dream bigger than you have in the past.
- Action: Create a vision board or detailed vision statement that represents your future self.

Gratitude Tip: Express gratitude for future opportunities that are awaiting you.

Day 26

Date: _____

Day 27

Date: _____

Continuous Growth

"Be not afraid of growing slowly; be afraid only of standing still." - Chinese Proverb

Reflection Prompt:

What are some ways you can continue to grow and excel after completing your journey?

Daily Intentions and Actions:

- Intentions: Set an intention for continuous growth.
- Action: Create meaningful goals and an action plan for success.

Gratitude Tip: Express appreciation for the ways you have grown during your journey.

Day 27

Date: _____

Day 28

Date: _____

Giving Back

"The best way to find yourself is to lose yourself in the service of others." Mahatma Ghandi

Reflection Prompt:

How can you use your sensitivity to honor your empowered self while helping others?

Daily Intentions and Actions:

- Intentions: Set an intention to be of service from a place of strength.
- Action: Offer meaningful support to someone. Reflect on any insights given.

Gratitude Tip: Express gratitude for the opportunity to be of service to others.

Day 28

Date: _____

Day 29

Date: _____

Mindful Reflection

"Life takes on meaning when you become motivated, set goals, and charge after them in an unstoppable manner.
Les Brown

Reflection Prompt:

Reflect on your time in the sanctuary. What has changed for you? What are some ways you have grown stronger?

Daily Intentions and Actions:

- Intentions: Set an intention to honor your transformation.
- Action: Write a letter to your future self detailing your experiences in the sanctuary and how they led to your successful life.

Gratitude Tip: Express gratitude for your sacred journey and transformation.

Day 29

Date: _____

Day 30

Date: _____

Process Day

"Find the joy in the journey. Success isn't simply about reaching a destination, but instead about learning from life's highs and lows and growing stronger with each breath."
Shenita Sanders

Congratulations, my friend. You've crossed the finish line! You have completed your journey of self-discovery and mastery. This moment is truly significant, and I hope you are taking the time to celebrate your incredible achievement.

Today, reflect on your journey and recognize the invaluable insights you've gained. Acknowledge the moments that have enhanced your time in the sanctuary and how they can be used for future inspiration. Take a moment to fully appreciate the person you have become and the abundance that now flows into your life and affects how you show up in the world.

I will conclude our sacred journey with this prayer. May you be happy, may you be well, and may love always find its way to you. Namaste.

Day 30

Date: _____

Date: _____

Date: _____

Date: _____

Date: _____

Date: _____

Date: _____

Date: _____

Date: _____

Date: _____

Date: _____

Date: _____

Date: _____

Date: _____

Date: _____

Date: _____

Date: _____

Date:

Date: _____

Date: _____

Date: _____

Date: _____

Date: _____

Date: _____

Date: _____

Date: _____

Date: _____

Date: _____

Made in the USA
Columbia, SC
01 November 2024